Rosemary Wells

CHARLES LE TIMIDE

l'école des loisirs
11, rue de Sèvres, Paris 6ᵉ

Adapté de l'américain par Alain Broutin
© 1988, l'école des loisirs, Paris, pour l'édition en langue française
© 1988, Rosemary Wells
Titre original : « Shy Charles » (Dial Books, New York)
Composition : Sereg, Paris (Goudy 16/22)
Loi numéro 49.956 du 16 juillet 1949 sur les publications destinées
à la jeunesse : septembre 1988
Dépôt légal : décembre 1990
Imprimé en France par Aubin Imprimeur à Poitiers

Charles était aussi heureux que possible.

Mais il ne jouait avec personne,
ne parlait pas à sa voisine...

... et avait peur de répondre au téléphone.

«Tu vas être content», lui dit sa maman.
«Nous allons dire bonjour à notre amie l'épicière.
Nous achèterons une galette de pommes de terre
et nous dirons au revoir en repartant.»

«Quelle matinée magnifique!» dit Madame Lemarchand.
«Et ce grand garçon, est-ce qu'il aime les friandises?»

«Charles, qu'est-ce qu'on dit?» lui chuchota sa maman.
«On dit merci», dit en riant Madame Lemarchand.

«Maintenant, dis au revoir!»
Mais Charles alla se fourrer dans un grand sac de farine.
«Au revoir et gros bisous», cria Madame Lemarchand.
«Tu m'embrasseras plus tard, quand tu seras grand.»

Sa maman lui dit: «Charles, je suis très fâchée!
tu ne dis jamais ni au revoir, ni merci.
Je suis beaucoup trop gentille,
une autre maman t'aurait donné la fessée.»

Son papa lui dit: «Charles, tu n'es pas poli!
Je suis fatigué de ta désobéissance. Désormais, tu iras jouer
au football ou tu prendras des cours de danse.»

Le mardi suivant, Charles enfila son collant neuf.

Madame Lafleur s'écria: «Comme tu es mignon!»
Charles ne lui répondit ni oui, ni non.

Pendant une semaine, il fit semblant de dormir.

Charles n'était pas un danseur étoile.

Alors son papa l'emmena dans un magasin
pour acheter une tenue de football américain.
Sur le maillot écarlate, il y avait des épaulettes.
Le casque était décoré avec des ailes argentées.

Son papa lui dit: «Tu vas jouer comme un champion.
Tu vas courir vite, plus vite que l'éclair,
tu dépasseras tous tes adversaires,
c'est toi qui feras gagner ton équipe.»

Charles tremblait comme une feuille.
«Salut!» rugit l'entraîneur, «moi, je m'appelle Fred!»

«Il n'a pas l'air très en forme,
je crois qu'il vaut mieux qu'il rentre et qu'il dorme.»

Son papa lui dit : «Charles, tu n'es qu'un poltron.
Tu me fais l'effet d'un sandwich sans pain,
sans beurre et sans jambon, mais avec un cornichon.
Comment te débrouilleras-tu quand tu iras à l'école,
et pour trouver du travail, et pour te marier?»
Charles s'était assis par terre et pleurait comme une fontaine.

Il fallut le transporter.

Alors son papa lui murmura à l'oreille:
«Une baby-sitter va venir ce soir,
tu la connais bien, c'est Madame Martin,
tu seras content de la voir.»

Puis le soleil se coucha.

A six heures, les parents de Charles sortirent et la baby-sitter arriva.

Aussitôt, Charles détala dans l'escalier.

«Reste avec moi, mon trésor», cria Madame Martin.

Dans sa chambre, Charles jouait au cosmonaute.
Avec des chaises il s'était construit un vaisseau spatial.
Mais soudain, patatras! une catastrophe arriva.

Madame Martin était tombée dans l'escalier.

Charles la tira jusqu'au canapé.
«Restez bien calme», lui dit-il.

Il lui apporta une couverture et une tasse de chocolat.
Puis il appela l'hôpital et les pompiers.

«Charles m'a sauvé la vie», dit Madame Martin en gémissant.
«C'est un prince charmant, une perle rare, un héros!»

Alors chacun s'écria: «Bravo Charles, c'est très bien!»
Mais Charles ne répondit...

... rien.

GRAPHIC BIOGRAPHIES

MARTIN LUTHER KING JR

THE LIFE OF A CIVIL RIGHTS LEADER

by
GARY JEFFREY
illustrated by
CHRIS FORSEY

W
FRANKLIN WATTS
LONDON • SYDNEY

First published in 2007 by Franklin Watts

Franklin Watts
338 Euston Road
London NW1 3BH

Franklin Watts Australia
Level 17/207 Kent Street
Sydney, NSW 2000

A CIP catalogue record for this book is available from the British Library.

ISBN: 978 0 7496 7783 1

Franklin Watts is a division of Hachette Children's Books.

GRAPHIC BIOGRAPHIES: MARTIN LUTHER KING JR. produced for Franklin Watts
by David West Children's Books, 7 Princeton Court, 55 Felsham Road,
London SW15 1AZ

Designed and produced by
David West 🏃🏃 Children's Books

Editor: Dominique Crowley
Photo Research: Victoria Cook

Photo credits:
page 4 Library of Congress; page 5 (top, middle, bottom) Library of Congress; page 6
(top, bottom) Library of Congress; page 7 (top, bottom) Library of Congress; page 44
SIPA/REX FEATURES; page 45 Library of Congress

Printed in China

CONTENTS

WHO'S WHO

 **Martin Luther King Jr** (1929–1968) Born in Atlanta and the son of a preacher, King worked to improve the lives of minority groups, especially those of African Americans in the South.

 **Coretta Scott King** (1927–2006) The wife of Martin Luther King Jr and mother of their four children, Coretta studied music at Boston University, where she and King first met. She was also involved in civil rights work.

 **President John F. Kennedy** (1917–1963) Kennedy was the US president who worked with King regarding African Americans' civil rights.

 **Ralph Abernathy** (1926–1990) Baptist Church pastor and close friend of Martin Luther King Jr, Abernathy was heavily involved in King's campaign to achieve equal rights for everyone.

 **Rosa Parks** (1913–2005) Parks refused to give up her seat on a bus to a white person, as required by law. Her action caused the Montgomery Bus Boycott of 1955.

 **President Lyndon Baines Johnson** (1907–1973) Johnson was the 36th president of the United States. He championed civil rights.

FREEDOM'S PROMISE

*A*t the end of the American Civil War in 1865, African Americans were no longer slaves but they still weren't free. How would they live successfully in a world that was hostile towards them?

FREEDOM'S FATHER
In 1862, during the American Civil War, President Lincoln passed a law that freed slaves in the United States.

FALSE FREEDOM

Changes to the American Constitution between 1866 and 1877 gave black people new rights. They were allowed to vote and to take an active part in the political process. They were also given the right to purchase the land of their former owners, and to use all public buildings.

Before the Civil War, certain states had laws that prevented education of slaves. These states were known as 'slave states' and included Louisiana and Alabama, among others, in the South. After the Civil War, former slaves crowded into newly built schools to learn to read and write. Racists, however, were quietly uniting against them, waiting to strike out openly.

They got their chance in 1883 when the Supreme Court ruled that the Civil Rights Act of 1875 was unconstitutional. Following this, Southern states passed laws that kept black people apart from white people. Then, in 1890, a law in Louisiana stated that black people must ride in separate railroad cars from whites. African Americans in Louisiana challenged the law. A local judge and, later, the US Supreme Court, ruled against them. Acceptance of what came to be known as the Jim Crow laws had begun.

BOOKER T. WASHINGTON

EARLY CAMPAIGNERS

The period from the 1890s to the start of World War I in 1914 was a difficult time for those fighting for racial equality. Liberty, won after the Civil War, was soon lost as African Americans were not always treated equally by white society. Racial violence was also at an all-time high. Yet, during these dark times, two strong leaders emerged.

Booker T. Washington was born into slavery in Virginia and had achieved success through hard work. He believed that education was the way to create a proud and strong black society that could exist alongside a white one.

William Edward Burghardt Dubois was born in Massachusetts and was a university graduate. He was the first African American to be elected to the board of the National Association for the Advancement of Colored People (NAACP). This organisation, founded in 1910 by both black and white people, believed in racial equality and fought for the civil rights of black Americans.

W. E. B. DUBOIS

THE JIM CROW LAWS

Named after a nineteenth-century stage character who mocked black people, the Jim Crow laws kept African Americans divided from white citizens. They promoted separate entrances and facilities in waiting rooms, cinemas, restaurants and even at drinking fountains. Usually, the areas for African Americans were of a much lower standard than those for the use of their white counterparts.

OUT OF SIGHT
A man uses the 'coloured' entrance to a Mississippi cinema in 1939.

AMERICA DIVIDED

In 1941, President Franklin D. Roosevelt issued an executive order to allow the full participation of African Americans in the armed forces during World War II. This was at the request of a civil rights pressure group, and its victory made a big impression on the rest of African-American society.

RETURNING HOME

Southern African-American veterans returning from World War II were often unwilling to suffer the humiliation of segregation, as they had before the war. Some whites, especially white supremacist groups like the Ku Klux Klan, felt that African Americans were an inferior race. As a result, acts of violence, including hangings in the South, were perpetrated against Blacks. This led to greater urgency among those fighting against racism, such as Martin Luther King Jr.

THE FIGHT FOR EQUAL RIGHTS

Working on a school segregation case in Charleston, in the state of South Carolina, NAACP lawyers convinced the Supreme Court to ban segregation in schools. The 1954 case marked a turning point in the fight for equal rights for African Americans. The decision de-segregated Southern schools in 1957.

PROUD VETERANS
African Americans had fought and shed blood for four years alongside white people in World War II. Now they wanted equality at home.

FIRST VICTORY
African Americans celebrate news of the 1954 Brown vs Board of Education *case.*

THE BROTHERHOOD RISES

The first African-American leader to use mass protest tactics against segregation laws was the labour leader A. Philip Randolph. In 1941, he threatened to lead a march on Washington, DC, with hundreds of thousands of people to protest job discrimination in the military. The march never actually took place, but Randolph did eventually get his day. He was a co-organiser of one of the most famous marches for civil rights in American history, the March on Washington in 1963.

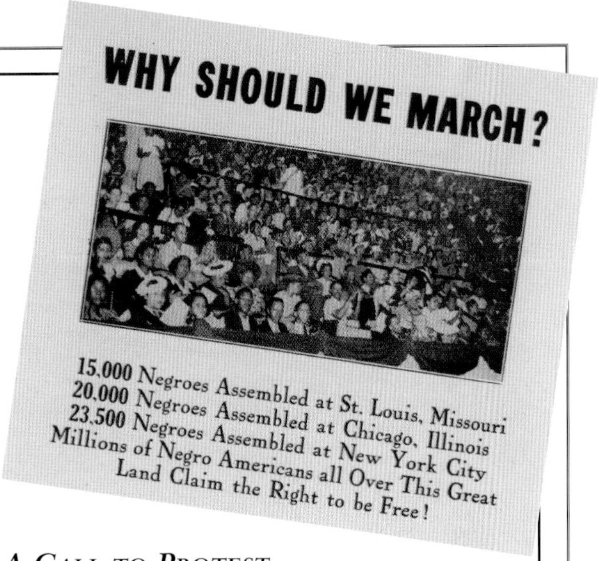

WHY SHOULD WE MARCH?

15.000 Negroes Assembled at St. Louis, Missouri
20.000 Negroes Assembled at Chicago, Illinois
23.500 Negroes Assembled at New York City
Millions of Negro Americans all Over This Great
Land Claim the Right to be Free!

A CALL TO PROTEST
This flier was produced to encourage as many African Americans as possible to participate in the proposed march on Washington, DC.

A PREACHER'S SON

Martin Luther King Jr was born on 15 January 1929, in Atlanta, Georgia. At the time, Atlanta was heavily segregated. King would grow up to be one of the greatest preachers and speakers in history, taking after his father, Martin Luther King Sr, the pastor of a local church.

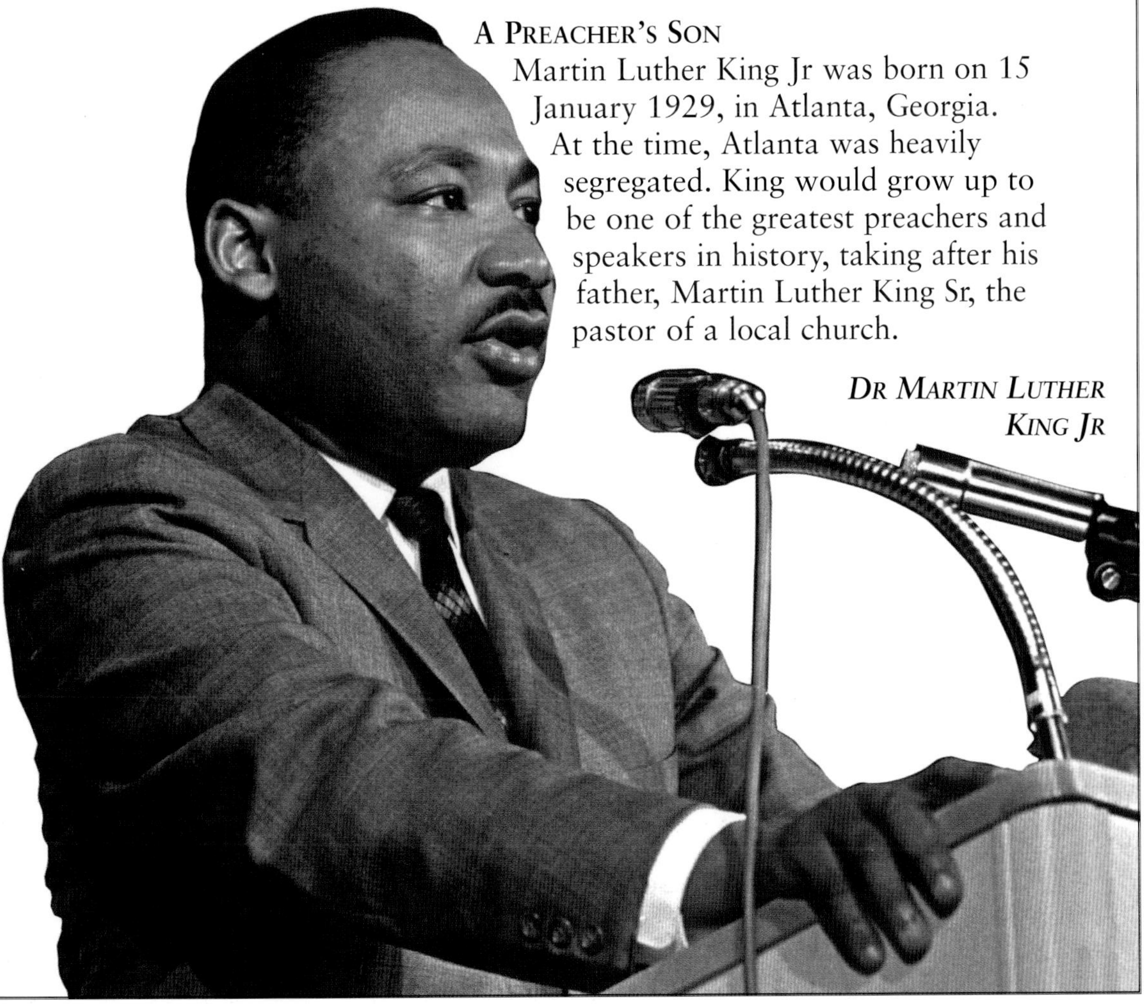

DR MARTIN LUTHER KING JR

MARTIN LUTHER KING JR

THE LIFE OF A CIVIL RIGHTS LEADER

EBENEZER BAPTIST CHURCH, ATLANTA, GEORGIA, 1934.

LET ME HEAR YOU SAY HALLELUJAH!

HALLELUJAH!

I STILL CAN'T HEAR YOU!

MARTIN, YOUR DADDY IS SUCH A FINE PREACHER!

LATER, AT THE KINGS' HOUSE ON AUBURN AVENUE IN ATLANTA, KING PLAYED WITH HIS BEST FRIEND FROM ACROSS THE STREET.

MARTIN STARTS SCHOOL TOMORROW. MAYBE WE SHOULD TELL HIM ABOUT...

NO! HE'LL LEARN IT SOON ENOUGH.

THE NEXT DAY AT THE LOCAL SCHOOL, KING LOOKED IN VAIN FOR HIS PLAY FRIEND.

AFTER SCHOOL, HE WENT TO HIS FRIEND'S HOUSE.

MY BOY CAN'T PLAY WITH YOU ANYMORE.

WHY NOT?

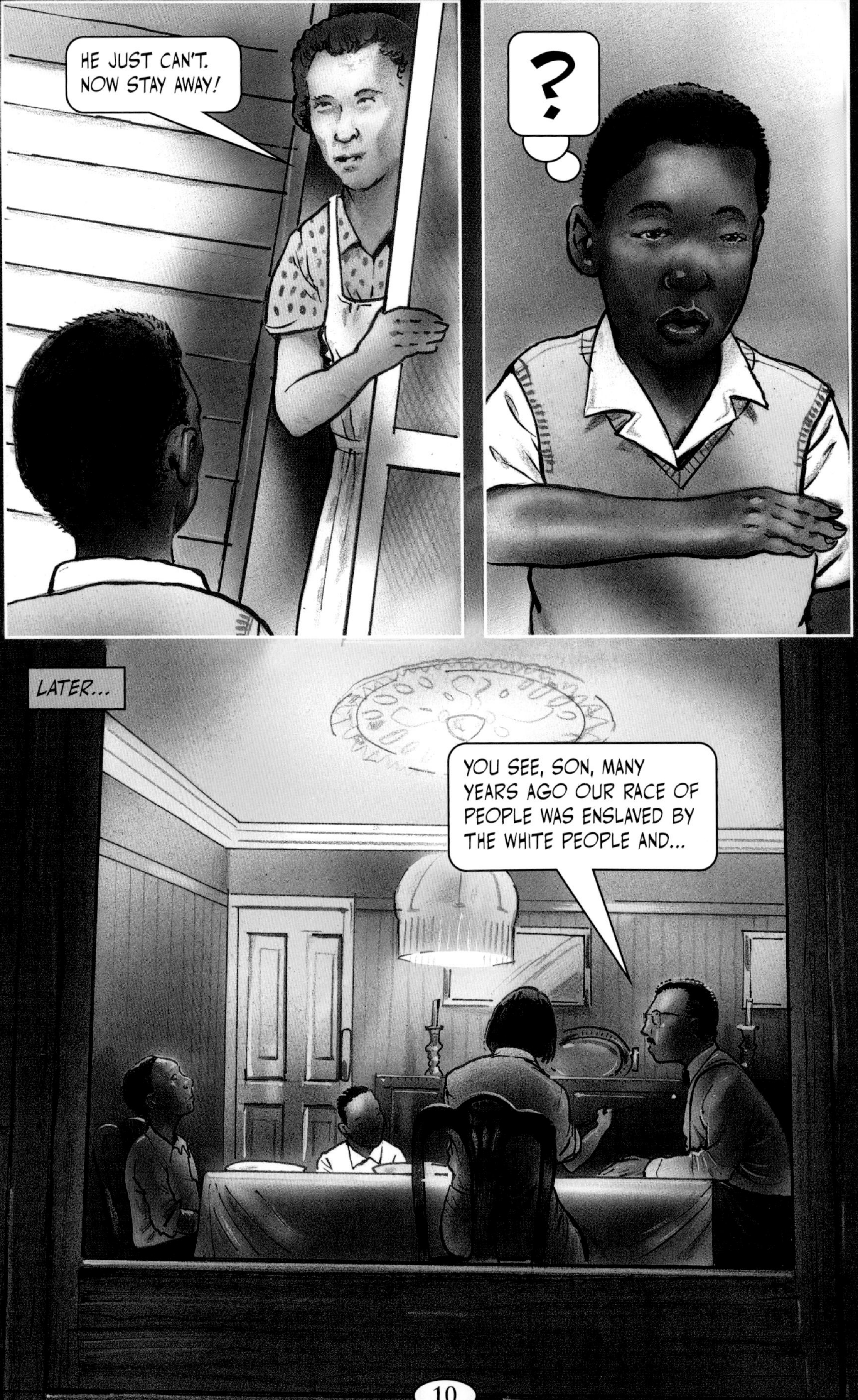

HE JUST CAN'T. NOW STAY AWAY!

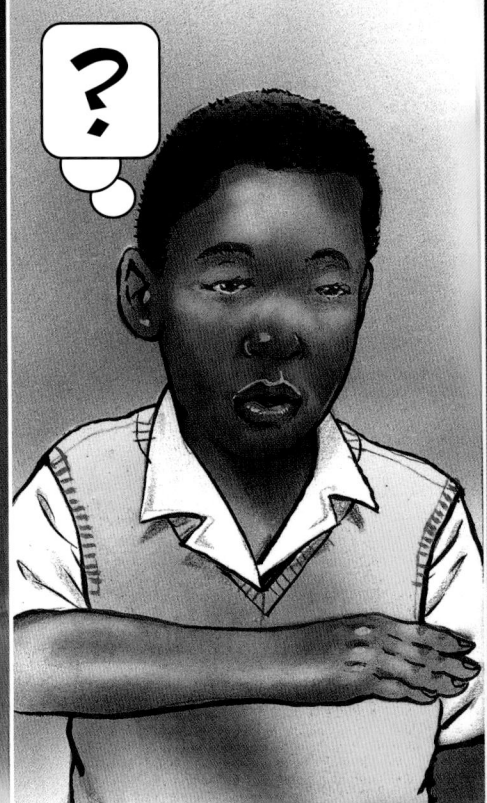

?

LATER...

YOU SEE, SON, MANY YEARS AGO OUR RACE OF PEOPLE WAS ENSLAVED BY THE WHITE PEOPLE AND...

KING'S FATHER WENT ON TO EXPLAIN THE AMERICAN CIVIL WAR AND THE FREEING OF THE AFRICAN-AMERICAN SLAVES BY PRESIDENT ABRAHAM LINCOLN.

...BUT EVEN THOUGH WE ARE FREE, SOME PEOPLE KEEP US BELOW THEM BY KEEPING US APART FROM THEM.

YOU MUST NEVER FEEL THAT YOU ARE LESS THAN ANYBODY ELSE.

YOU MUST ALWAYS FEEL THAT YOU ARE SOMEBODY SPECIAL!

GROWING UP IN ATLANTA, KING SAW SIGNS OF SEGREGATION EVERYWHERE IN THE CITY.

PUBLIC TOILETS, LUNCH COUNTERS AND EVEN DRINKING FOUNTAINS WERE CLOSED TO PEOPLE OF HIS SKIN COLOUR, OR HAD SEPARATE ENTRANCES AND AREAS.

KING DID VERY WELL IN SCHOOL AND SHOWED AN EARLY TALENT FOR PUBLIC SPEAKING. DURING ELEVENTH GRADE, HE TOOK PART IN A SPEAKING CONTEST AT ANOTHER SCHOOL AND WAS TRAVELLING HOME WITH A TEACHER WHEN...

MARTIN, YOU WON! YOUR PARENTS WILL BE SO PROUD!

YOU FOLKS HAVE TO STAND UP. THESE PEOPLE NEED TO SIT!

WHY SHOULD WE? WE'RE ALREADY IN THE COLOURED SECTION.

WHY YOU...!

MARTIN, PLEASE, DON'T MAKE A FUSS.

KING AND HIS TEACHER STOOD THE REST OF THE WAY HOME BUT ANGER BOILED IN HIS HEART.

IF I ACCEPT THAT IT'S THE SYSTEM THAT TURNS PEOPLE INTO RACISTS, THEN HOW DO I CHANGE THE SYSTEM?

AT CROZIER KING ATTENDED A LECTURE ABOUT THE INDIAN LEADER FOR PEACE, MAHATMA GHANDI.

GHANDI USED THE POWER OF LOVE AND TRUTH TO CREATE SOCIAL CHANGE.

LIKE GHANDI, I MUST CHANNEL MY ANGER INTO A POSITIVE AND CREATIVE FORCE!

HE READ ALL THE BOOKS HE COULD FIND ON GHANDI, PARTICULARLY ONE CALLED 'THE POWER OF NON-VIOLENCE'.

REACTING TO HATRED WITH HATRED ONLY ADDS TO THE **BITTERNESS** OF THE WORLD. ONLY WHEN THE CHAIN OF HATRED IS CUT, CAN **BROTHERHOOD** BEGIN.

IN 1951, KING FINISHED AT THE TOP OF HIS CLASS AND WON A SCHOLARSHIP TO BOSTON UNIVERSITY, TO STUDY FOR A PH.D. IN APPLIED RELIGION. THERE, HE MET CORETTA SCOTT.

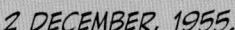

2 DECEMBER, 1955.

YOU MAKE IT EASY ON YOURSELVES AND GIVE UP YOUR SEATS NOW.

YOU THERE! ARE YOU GOING TO GET UP OR WHAT?

HER NAME IS ROSA PARKS, AND, GET THIS, THE BUS DRIVER **DEMANDED** HER ARREST!

NO, I'M NOT.

WELL, IT LOOKS LIKE WE'VE GOT OUR CASE!

BY THAT EVENING, THE LOCAL LEADERS HAD FORMED THE MONTGOMERY IMPROVEMENT ASSOCIATION (MIA) AND ELECTED MARTIN LUTHER KING JR AS THEIR LEADER. AT HOLT STREET BAPTIST CHURCH, HE SPOKE AT THE FIRST MASS MEETING.

WE ALL KNOW WHAT HAPPENED TO ROSA PARKS AND OF ALL THE INDIGNITIES WE BLACKS HAVE SUFFERED ON THE BUSES.

IF WE PROTEST COURAGEOUSLY, AND YET WITH DIGNITY AND LOVE, WHEN THE HISTORY BOOKS ARE WRITTEN, THEN SOMEBODY WILL HAVE TO SAY...

...THERE LIVED A RACE OF PEOPLE WHO HAD THE MORAL COURAGE TO STAND UP FOR THEIR RIGHTS, AND FOR WHAT THEY BELIEVED!

HIS SPEECH ELECTRIFIED THE CONGREGATION. A LIST OF DEMANDS, TO BE SENT TO THE AUTHORITIES, WAS APPROVED BY THE CROWD. THE FIGHT WAS ON.

LATER, THE CITY DECLARED THE BUS BOYCOTT ILLEGAL. KING WAS AMONG EIGHTY-NINE AFRICAN AMERICANS ARRESTED FOR THEIR PART IN THE PROTEST. BUT THE MIA KEPT THE BOYCOTT GOING, FIRST WITH CHEAP TAXIS, AND THEN WITH A CARPOOL. THE CITY ASKED THE COURT TO SHUT DOWN THE CARPOOL.

7089

IN NOVEMBER, IT LOOKED AS THOUGH THE CITY WAS GOING TO WIN, UNTIL...

THE SUPREME COURT RULES THAT ALABAMA'S SEGREGATION LAWS ARE...UNCONSTITUTIONAL!

HALLELUJAH, BROTHER!

BEFORE LONG...

LOOK AT THAT. COLOURED AND WHITE FOLKS ARE SIDE BY SIDE!

YES, RALPH, A SMALL VICTORY...A BEGINNING!

23

YOU LOOK WORRIED ABOUT MARTIN, BROTHER RALPH.

IT'S A LOT FOR ONE MAN TO DO...

...TO BE A GOOD HUSBAND AND AN ATTENTIVE FATHER TO HIS CHILDREN...

...SET UP AND BE PRESIDENT OF THE SCLC...*

...AND WRITE A BOOK!

*SOUTHERN CHRISTIAN LEADERSHIP CONFERENCE

'STRIDE TOWARD FREEDOM: THE MONTGOMERY STORY' WAS PUBLISHED IN THE AUTUMN. ON 20 SEPTEMBER, KING WAS AT A BOOK SIGNING IN NEW YORK, WHEN...

MARTIN LUTHER KING, I'VE BEEN AFTER YOU FOR FIVE YEARS.

WHAT?

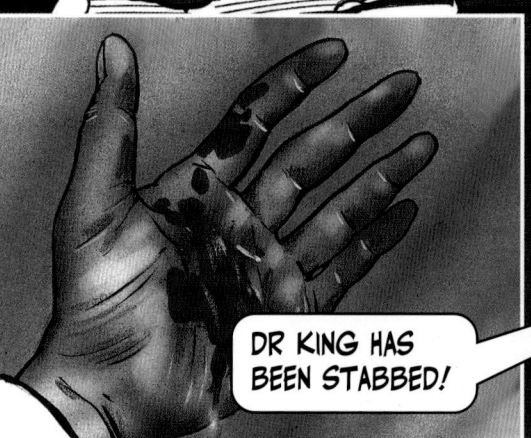

DR KING HAS BEEN STABBED!

LATER, AT HARLEM HOSPITAL, NEW YORK...

THE POLICE ARE SAYING SHE WAS A LONE MADWOMAN.

THE OBJECT LOOKS LIKE A LETTER OPENER AND IT'S JAMMED IN TIGHTLY.

DR MAYNARD, ARE YOU READY TO MAKE THE INCISION?

CONCENTRATE, EVERYONE. THIS IS A CRITICAL STAGE IN THE OPERATION...

LATER...

I GUESS I OWE YOU MY LIFE, DOCTOR.

YOU WERE LUCKY. THE TIP OF THE BLADE WAS TOUCHING YOUR HEART. IF YOU'D SNEEZED JUST ONCE...

FATE OBVIOUSLY HAS OTHER PLANS FOR ME!

20 MAY, MARTIN LUTHER KING JR'S NEW HOUSE IN ATLANTA.

HERE IN MONTGOMERY, A THOUSAND ARMED WHITES ARE ATTACKING THE FREEDOM RIDERS WITHOUT ANY POLICE INTERFERENCE WHATSOEVER.

RALPH? **RALPH!** THIS IS MARTIN. I'M COMING DOWN TO MONTGOMERY RIGHT AWAY!

THAT EVENING AT ABERNATHY'S CHURCH, KING TRIED TO REASON WITH A WHITE MOB. THE STRUGGLE WOULD BE KNOWN AS THE BATTLE OF MONTGOMERY.

PEOPLE, LISTEN TO...WHAT THE...

FZZZZT!

DR KING, LOOK OUT!

ONLY THE ARRIVAL OF FEDERAL MARSHALS, SENT BY THE US GOVERNMENT, STOPPED THE CHURCH BEING STORMED.

IN 1963, AFTER THE US GOVERNMENT BROUGHT AN END TO INTERSTATE BUS SEGREGATION, THE SCLC WENT TO BIRMINGHAM, ALABAMA. HUNDREDS OF MARCHERS, INCLUDING KING, WERE IMPRISONED BY POLICE CHIEF BULL CONNOR. FROM HIS PRISON CELL, KING WROTE 'A LETTER FROM BIRMINGHAM JAIL', WHICH WAS PUBLISHED ALL OVER THE WORLD.

LATE APRIL, SCLC HEADQUARTERS, BIRMINGHAM.

MARTIN, WHERE ARE WE GOING TO GET OUR MARCHERS **FROM?** EVERYONE'S IN JAIL!

HMMM...

3 MAY, 1963. IN BIRMINGHAM 2,500 CHILDREN JOINED KING AND OTHERS ON A MARCH INTO THE CITY.

DON'T GET TIRED. DON'T GET BITTER. **ARE YOU TIRED?**

NO!

BLOCKING THEIR WAY WAS CHIEF BULL CONNOR.

AS KING LOOKED ON, REVEREND BILLUPS ADDRESSED THE BLOCKADE.

WE'RE NOT TURNING BACK. WE HAVEN'T DONE ANYTHING WRONG. HOW DO YOU FEEL DOING THESE THINGS?

BRING ON YOUR DOGS. BEAT US UP. TURN ON YOUR HOSES. WE ARE NOT GOING TO RETREAT.

TURN ON THE HOSES! TURN ON THE HOSES!

CONNOR'S MEN STOOD ASIDE AND LET THE CHILDREN THROUGH. THE SIGHT OF THE MEN TREATING THE CHILDREN WITH CARE, AND REFUSING TO FOLLOW CONNOR'S ORDERS, MADE KING ECSTATIC.

THE TIDE HAD TURNED. ON 10 MAY, A GROUP OF LEADING BIRMINGHAM BUSINESSMEN AGREED TO END THEIR SEGREGATIONIST PRACTICES THROUGHOUT THE CITY.

THE CITY OF BIRMINGHAM HAS REACHED AN ACCORD WITH ITS CONSCIENCE. IT IS AN EXAMPLE OF PROGRESSIVE RACE RELATIONS.

ON 11 JUNE, 1963, PRESIDENT KENNEDY ADDRESSED THE NATION.

I'M GOING TO ASK THE CONGRESS TO MAKE A COMMITMENT TO THE PROPOSITION THAT RACE HAS NO PLACE IN AMERICAN LIFE.

THE BILL WOULD EFFECTIVELY OUTLAW SEGREGATION IN PUBLIC FACILITIES ACROSS AMERICA.

ON 22 JUNE, KING MET WITH THE PRESIDENT.

NOW IS **NOT** THE RIGHT TIME FOR A MARCH ON WASHINGTON, DR KING.

WE WANT THE CIVIL RIGHTS BILL TO SUCCEED IN CONGRESS. A MASS DEMONSTRATION WOULD BE ILL-TIMED.

FRANKLY, I HAVE NEVER TAKEN PART IN ANY DIRECT-ACTION MOVEMENT THAT DID **NOT** SEEM ILL-TIMED. MANY PEOPLE THOUGHT THAT **BIRMINGHAM** WAS ILL-TIMED.

I TAKE YOUR POINT, BUT TO LOSE THE FIGHT IN CONGRESS WOULD BE A TERRIBLE THING. IT COULD BRING THE WHOLE ADMINISTRATION **DOWN.** WE'RE UP TO OUR NECKS IN THIS THING!

MR PRESIDENT, THE AFRICAN AMERICANS' PATIENCE IS AT AN END. A MASS MARCH WOULD BE A WAY FOR MY PEOPLE TO CHANNEL THEIR ANGER – A CALM, **CONSTRUCTIVE** WAY FOR THEM TO EXPRESS THEIR GRIEVANCES.

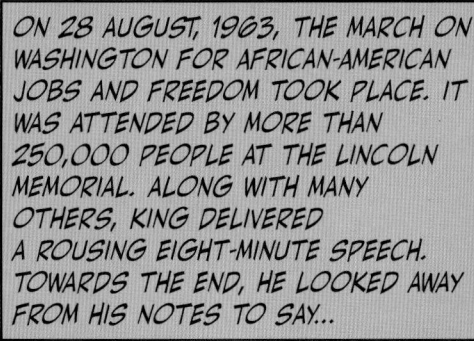

ON 28 AUGUST, 1963, THE MARCH ON WASHINGTON FOR AFRICAN-AMERICAN JOBS AND FREEDOM TOOK PLACE. IT WAS ATTENDED BY MORE THAN 250,000 PEOPLE AT THE LINCOLN MEMORIAL. ALONG WITH MANY OTHERS, KING DELIVERED A ROUSING EIGHT-MINUTE SPEECH. TOWARDS THE END, HE LOOKED AWAY FROM HIS NOTES TO SAY...

I HAVE A DREAM TODAY.

I HAVE A DREAM THAT ONE DAY, DOWN IN ALABAMA WITH ITS FIERCE RACISTS...THAT ONE DAY, RIGHT THERE IN ALABAMA...

...LITTLE BLACK BOYS AND BLACK GIRLS WILL BE ABLE TO JOIN HANDS WITH LITTLE WHITE BOYS AND WHITE GIRLS AS SISTERS AND BROTHERS.

I HAVE A *DREAM* TODAY.

ATLANTA, 22 NOVEMBER, 1963.

WE INTERRUPT THIS PROGRAM WITH TERRIBLE NEWS...PRESIDENT KENNEDY HAS BEEN SHOT!

THE THIRTY-FIFTH PRESIDENT OF THE UNITED STATES IS DEAD FROM A SNIPER'S BULLET.

AS THE PRESIDENT'S BODY ARRIVES BACK IN WASHINGTON, VICE PRESIDENT LYNDON B. JOHNSON IS BEING SWORN IN.

CORETTA, I DON'T THINK I'M GOING TO LIVE TO REACH FORTY.

MARTIN DON'T SAY SUCH A THING!

I MEAN IT. THIS IS A SICK NATION. I DON'T SEE HOW I CAN SURVIVE.

ON 10 DECEMBER, 1964, IN OSLO, NORWAY, MARTIN LUTHER KING JR ACCEPTED THE NOBEL PEACE PRIZE FOR HIS CIVIL RIGHTS WORK.

HE HAD HELPED COMBAT RACIAL SEGREGATION, BUT IT TROUBLED HIM THAT OVER HALF THE AFRICAN AMERICANS IN THE SOUTH STILL LACKED THE RIGHT TO VOTE.

A FEW DAYS LATER, AT THE WHITE HOUSE.

NOW IS NOT THE RIGHT TIME TO PUSH THROUGH OUR NEGRO VOTING RIGHTS BILL, DR KING.

IT'S BEEN HARD ENOUGH JUST GETTING KENNEDY'S CIVIL RIGHTS BILL THROUGH CONGRESS. YOU'LL HAVE TO WAIT UNTIL THE YEAR AFTER NEXT.

ALL RIGHT, PRESIDENT JOHNSON, WE'LL JUST HAVE TO LAUNCH OUR OWN BILL...ON THE STREETS!

AS THEY WALKED DEEPER INTO THE COUNTRY...

SEE THAT CHURCH, WITH ITS ROOF HALF OFF?

THAT IS WHY WE'RE MARCHING!

PEOPLE, MARTIN IS OUR BLACK MOSES SENT BY GOD TO LEAD US FROM THE WILDERNESS!

THAT'S **THE** MARTIN LUTHER KING! I HAVE KISSED **THE** MARTIN LUTHER KING!

ON 25 MARCH, KING LED 25,000 MARCHERS INTO MONTGOMERY. ON 6 AUGUST, 1965, PRESIDENT JOHNSON SIGNED A BILL INTO LAW THAT ALLOWED AFRICAN AMERICANS TO REGISTER TO VOTE.

IN 1967, KING BEGAN PLANNING A MASS DEMONSTRATION THAT WOULD TAKE PLACE IN WASHINGTON. THE ISSUE WOULD BE POVERTY AND THE PROTEST WOULD LAST THREE MONTHS AND INVOLVE HUNDREDS OF THOUSANDS OF PEOPLE.

WE WILL BRING THE CAPITOL TO A STANDSTILL AND **MAKE** THIS GOVERNMENT LISTEN AND RESPOND TO THE NEEDS OF THE POOR.

THE GREAT MARCH WAS PLANNED FOR SPRING 1968. BUT SOME AFRICAN AMERICANS WERE GROWING RESTLESS WITH THE SLOW PACE OF CHANGE.

THE LEADERS OF A BLACK YOUTH GROUP IN MEMPHIS, TENNESSEE, WERE NOT IMPRESSED WHEN THEY READ OF KING'S PLAN.

NON-VIOLENCE? DO THEY REALLY THINK THAT'S GOING TO CHANGE THE MINDS OF THE PEOPLE RUNNING THIS COUNTRY?

KING ISN'T GOING TO **GET** US ANYTHING. IF WE WANT OUR RIGHTS, WE'VE GOT TO **TAKE THEM!**

THE RIOT MADE THE NATIONAL PRESS.

'DR KING'S POSE AS THE LEADER OF A PEACEFUL MOVEMENT HAS BEEN SHATTERED.' BOY, THEY'RE REALLY DOING A NUMBER ON YOU, MARTIN.

I HAVE TO COME BACK AND PROVE THEM WRONG!

EVEN THOUGH THERE'S A PRICE ON YOUR HEAD?*

*ABERNATHY HAD HEARD A RUMOUR OF AN OFFER OF $50,000 FOR KING'S ASSASSINATION.

THE LORRAINE MOTEL, MEMPHIS, 4 APRIL. KING RETURNED TO LEAD ANOTHER MARCH FOR THE CITY WORKERS.

MARTIN, I'LL BE RIGHT OUT!

OK, RALPH. I'LL JUST WAIT HERE.

42

BANG!

OH, NO! MARTIN'S BEEN SHOT!

MARTIN, THIS IS ME, RALPH. DON'T BE AFRAID...DON'T...

THE END

THE PROMISED LAND

Martin Luther King Jr died on the operating table at St Joseph's Hospital in Memphis, at 7.05 PM on 4 April, 1968. Following the official announcement, feelings of grief, guilt and rage gripped America.

SHOCK WAVES

Riots in response to King's assassination erupted in 110 cities, including Washington, DC. Seventy-five thousand troops and national guardsmen had to be sent out to restore order. As tributes poured in from around the world, a massive manhunt was under way for the assassin.

James Earl Ray, an escaped convict, was finally arrested, tried and found guilty of King's murder. He was later sentenced to 99 years in prison without parole.

KING HONOURED

After an emotional service attended by

MASS MOURNING
More than 60,000 people travelled to Atlanta, Georgia, on 9 April, 1968, to attend Martin Luther King Jr's funeral. His coffin was carried through the city on a cart drawn by two mules to represent his planned campaign for the poor.

mourners of many races at Ebenezer Baptist Church in Atlanta, King's coffin was brought to Morehouse College. Here, a eulogy was delivered by his old tutor, Dr Benjamin Mays. 'Martin Luther faced the dogs, the police, jail, heavy criticism, and finally death; and he never carried a gun, not even a knife to defend himself. He had only his faith to rely on.'

FORCE OF LAW
President Lyndon B. Johnson signed into law the Civil Rights Act of 1965, a direct result of King's influence.

KING'S LEGACY
When Martin Luther King Jr died, America lost a great leader. Even now, he still serves as a role model for society.

It is hard for young people growing up in America today to fully imagine living in the segregated society of the 1960s. This is due, in a large part, to Martin Luther King Jr's efforts towards social equality.

King also worked tirelessly to ensure that African Americans would have the right to vote. This has led to African Americans becoming mayors, judges and prominent politicians. Modern-day figures such as Colin Powell and Condoleezza Rice have risen high in society thanks, in part, to Martin Luther King Jr.

SELECTED WRITINGS AND SPEECHES OF MARTIN LUTHER KING JR
The purity of his message, and the eloquent way he delivered it, give Martin Luther King Jr's words a powerful relevance today.

SPEECHES

MIA Mass Meeting at Holt Street Baptist Church (1955)

'Give Us the Ballot' (1957)

'I Have a Dream' (1963)

'I've Been to the Mountaintop' (1968)

'Beyond Vietnam' (1968)

WRITINGS

Stride Toward Freedom: The Montgomery Story (1958)

Strength to Love (1963)

'Letter from Birmingham Jail' (1963)

Why We Can't Wait (1964)

The Trumpet of Conscience (1968)

Where Do We Go From Here: Chaos or Community? (1968)

GLOSSARY

accord An agreement.

assassination Killing a person, often secretly, and always planned in advance. Assassinations are often carried out for political reasons.

civil war A war where divisions within a group fight each other. The American Civil War lasted from 1861 to 1865.

congregation A group of people at a church.

constitution An accepted law or custom, or set of laws and customs.

enroll To sign up.

equality When everyone is treated the same.

graduate A person who has passed all examinations in a university.

hostile Unfriendly towards someone.

humiliation Making fun of a person to cause embarrassment while destroying his or her self-respect and dignity.

illegal An action that breaks the law.

indignity An action that makes a person feel worthless.

Ku Klux Klan A organisation of white people who believe in white supremacy and who harass, and sometimes murder, non-white citizens.

moral An issue of right or wrong.

mourner An individual who is deeply upset following the death of another person.

non-violence When peace is used instead of war.

perpetrate To carry out or bring about an action or event that is either illegal or linked to a crime.

preacher Someone who gives a sermon as part of a religious service.

protest A solemn announcement or disagreement, either with a person or a law. A protest can be violent or non-violent.

racist Someone who believes that a person's race affects their character, and that differences between races lead to the people of some races being superior to others.

riot To harm people and destroy property out of anger.

segregation The splitting off of a certain group away from the rest of society.

sniper Someone who kills or injures others by shooting them with a gun, usually from a concealed place.

supremacist Someone who believes that he or she is better than others because of his or her race.

theology The study of religious beliefs.

unconstitutional When an action goes against accepted laws or customs.

under the wing To be guided or protected by another person who is typically older and has more experience.

veteran Somebody who has been doing something for a very long time.

FOR MORE INFORMATION

ORGANISATIONS

The King Center
449 Auburn Avenue, N.E.
Atlanta, GA 30312
(404) 526-8900
E-mail: information@thekingcenter.org
Website: http://www.thekingcenter.org/

National Civil Rights Museum
450 Mulberry Street
Memphis, TN 38103
(901) 521-9699
Website: http://www.civilrightsmuseum.org

FOR FURTHER READING

King Jr., Martin Luther, and Clayborne Carson (ed.). *The Autobiography of Martin Luther King Jr.* South Victoria, Australia: Warner Books, 2001.

King Jr., Martin Luther, Coretta Scott King, and Dexter Scott King. *The Martin Luther King, Jr. Companion: Quotations from the Speeches, Essays, and Books of Martin Luther King Jr.* New York, NY: St. Martin's Press, 1998.

Levine, Ellen, and Beth Peck (illustrator). *If You Lived at the Time of Martin Luther King.* New York, NY: Scholastic Paperbacks, 1994.

Marzollo, J. and Brian Pin Kney (illustrator). *Happy Birthday, Martin Luther King.* New York, NY: Scholastic Press, 1993.

Millender, Dharathula H. *Martin Luther King Jr.: Young Man with a Dream.* New York, NY: Aladdin, 1986.

Pepper, William F. *An Act of State: The Execution of Martin Luther King.* New York, NY: Verso, 2003.

INDEX